ECONOMIC TRANSFORMATION: QATAR'S PATH TO SELF-SUFFICIENCY AND DIVERSIFICATION

Table of Contents

1. **Introduction**

. The Vision for Economic Transformation

. Objectives of the Book

2. **Historical Context**

. Economic Foundations of Qatar

. Pre-oil Economy

. The Oil Boom and its Impact

3. **Vision 2030: The Blueprint for Transformation**

. Overview of Qatar National Vision 2030

. Pillars of Development: Economic, Social, Environmental, and Human

. Implementation Strategies and Milestones

4. **Economic Diversification Strategies**

. Rationale for Diversification

. Key Sectors for Diversification: Finance, Tourism, Manufacturing, Agriculture, and

Technology
- Government Policies and Initiatives
- Case Studies of Successful Diversification Efforts

5. **Developing Local Industries**
   - Importance of Local Industries for Self-Sufficiency
   - Key Local Industries: Energy, Petrochemicals, Construction, and Services
   - Support Mechanisms: Financial Incentives, Infrastructure Development, and Capacity Building

6. **Agricultural Self-Sufficiency**
   - Challenges of Food Security in Qatar
   - Innovations in Agriculture: Hydroponics, Vertical Farming, and Aquaponics
   - Government Programs and Private Sector Initiatives

7. **Technology and Innovation**
   - Role of Technology in Economic Transformation
   - Qatar's Technology Ecosystem: Startups, Incubators, and Research Centers
   - Case Studies of Technological Innovations

8. **Human Capital Development**
   - Education Reforms and Skills Training
   - Empowerment of Women and Youth
   - Strategies for Attracting and Retaining Talent

9. **Sustainability and Environmental Stewardship**
   - Integrating Sustainability into Economic Planning
   - Renewable Energy Initiatives

. Environmental Policies and Regulations

10.   **Trade and Investment**

.Enhancing Trade Relations

.Attracting Foreign Direct Investment

.Free Zones and Economic Zones

11.   **Challenges and Risks**

.Economic Volatility and Global Market Dynamics

.Geopolitical Risks

.Domestic Challenges: Infrastructure, Workforce, and Regulation

12.   **Future Outlook**

.Projections for Qatar's Economy

.Long-term Goals and Vision Beyond 2030

.Strategic Recommendations for Continued Growth and Stability

13.   **Conclusion**

.Summary of Key Points

.Final Thoughts on Qatar's Economic Transformation Journey

14.   **References**

.Bibliography

.List of Sources and Further Reading

CHAPTER 1:
INTRODUCTION

The Vision for Economic Transformation

The Vision for Economic Transformation

A Nation's Ambitious Vision

Qatar's vision for economic transformation is a cornerstone of its national strategy to ensure long-term sustainability, prosperity, and resilience. This vision is embedded in the Qatar National Vision 2030 (QNV 2030), which sets the framework for the country's developmental trajectory. QNV 2030 reflects Qatar's ambition to transition from an oil-dependent economy to a diversified, knowledge-based economy that is resilient to global economic shifts.

Key Objectives of Economic Transformation

1. **Diversification of the Economy**: Reducing dependency on hydrocarbon revenues by developing other key sectors such as finance, tourism, manufacturing, agriculture, and technology.

2. **Sustainable Development**: Ensuring that economic growth is achieved in harmony with environmental protection and social well-being.

3. **Enhancing Competitiveness**: Building a competitive economy through innovation, entrepreneurship, and an enabling business environment.

4. **Human Capital Development**: Investing in education, skills, and health to build a capable and motivated workforce.

5. **Social Cohesion**: Fostering an inclusive society that

promotes social justice, equal opportunities, and a high quality of life for all citizens.

Strategic Pillars of the Vision

Qatar's economic transformation is structured around four strategic pillars, each contributing to the overarching goals of QNV 2030:

1. **Economic Development**:
   - Promoting diversification and competitiveness.
   - Encouraging private sector growth and investment.
   - Developing infrastructure and industrial bases.
   - Enhancing trade relations and attracting foreign direct investment.

2. **Social Development**:
   - Building a just and cohesive society.
   - Improving healthcare and social services.
   - Promoting cultural identity and heritage.
   - Ensuring equal opportunities for all citizens, including women and youth.

3. **Environmental Development**:
   - Managing natural resources responsibly.
   - Investing in renewable energy sources.
   - Implementing sustainable urban planning and infrastructure projects.
   - Reducing environmental footprint through green technologies and practices.

4. **Human Development**:
   - Reforming the education system to meet future market needs.
   - Enhancing vocational and technical training programs.
   - Promoting research and innovation.

. Attracting and retaining talent to drive the knowledge economy.

Implementation Strategies

To realize the vision of economic transformation, Qatar has laid out a multi-faceted implementation strategy:

1. **Policy Reforms**: Introducing regulatory reforms to create a conducive environment for business and investment. This includes simplifying business procedures, protecting intellectual property, and ensuring fair competition.

2. **Public-Private Partnerships**: Encouraging collaboration between the government and private sector to leverage resources, expertise, and innovation for economic development projects.

3. **Investment in Infrastructure**: Developing world-class infrastructure to support economic activities, including transportation networks, industrial zones, and digital infrastructure.

4. **Innovation and Technology**: Fostering a culture of innovation by investing in research and development, supporting startups, and integrating advanced technologies across industries.

5. **Capacity Building**: Strengthening institutions and human capital through continuous education, training, and professional development programs.

Milestones and Progress

Since the launch of QNV 2030, Qatar has achieved significant milestones in its journey towards economic transformation:

1. **Infrastructure Development**: The construction of Hamad International Airport, the Doha Metro, and numerous road networks has enhanced connectivity and supported economic activities.

2. **Energy Sector Diversification**: Investments in solar

energy projects and the development of the Barzan Gas Project have diversified Qatar's energy portfolio.

3. **Financial Sector Growth**: The establishment of the Qatar Financial Centre and the Qatar Stock Exchange has positioned Doha as a regional financial hub.

Objectives of the Book

The primary objective of this book is to provide a comprehensive analysis of Qatar's journey towards economic transformation, focusing on the strategies employed, the progress made, and the challenges faced. It aims to offer insights into the country's vision for the future, highlighting key sectors that drive diversification and the innovative approaches taken to achieve economic self-sufficiency. The book is structured to achieve several key objectives:

1. **Documenting Qatar's Economic History and Evolution**:

   - To provide readers with a thorough understanding of Qatar's economic history, tracing the evolution from a pre-oil economy to a modern, oil-dependent state, and finally, to its current efforts towards diversification.

   - To highlight the significant milestones in Qatar's economic journey, including the discovery of oil, the subsequent economic boom, and the strategic shifts towards diversification.

2. **Explaining the Vision and Strategies for Economic Diversification**:

   - To detail the Qatar National Vision 2030 (QNV 2030) and its strategic pillars, emphasizing the importance of economic diversification for long-term stability and growth.

   - To examine the specific sectors identified

for diversification, such as finance, tourism, manufacturing, agriculture, and technology, and the rationale behind their selection.

3. **Analyzing Government Policies and Initiatives**:

. To explore the various policies and initiatives introduced by the Qatari government to support economic diversification and self-sufficiency.

. To assess the effectiveness of these policies and initiatives in achieving the desired economic outcomes.

4. **Highlighting Key Sectors and Industries**:

. To provide an in-depth analysis of the key sectors and industries driving Qatar's economic transformation, including case studies of successful diversification efforts.

. To discuss the role of local industries in achieving self-sufficiency and reducing dependency on imports.

5. **Exploring Technological and Agricultural Innovations**:

. To examine the role of technology and innovation in Qatar's economic transformation, highlighting successful technological advancements and their impact on various sectors.

. To analyze the challenges and innovations in achieving agricultural self-sufficiency, including the adoption of modern farming techniques like hydroponics, vertical farming, and aquaponics.

6. **Assessing Human Capital Development**:

. To evaluate Qatar's efforts in human capital

development, including education reforms, skills training, and the empowerment of women and youth.

. To discuss strategies for attracting and retaining talent to support the knowledge-based economy.

7. **Emphasizing Sustainability and Environmental Stewardship**:

. To highlight Qatar's commitment to integrating sustainability into its economic planning and development.

. To explore renewable energy initiatives, environmental policies, and regulations aimed at promoting sustainable development.

8. **Understanding Trade and Investment Dynamics**:

. To analyze Qatar's efforts to enhance trade relations and attract foreign direct investment (FDI).

. To discuss the role of free zones and economic zones in fostering trade and investment.

9. **Identifying Challenges and Risks**:

. To identify and discuss the challenges and risks faced by Qatar in its economic transformation journey, including economic volatility, geopolitical risks, and domestic challenges.

. To propose strategies for mitigating these challenges and ensuring sustained economic growth.

10. **Projecting the Future Outlook**:

.To provide projections for Qatar's economy

based on current trends and strategic initiatives.

. To outline long-term goals and vision beyond 2030, offering strategic recommendations for continued growth and stability.

11.   **Inspiring Other Nations**:

. To serve as a case study and inspiration for other nations aspiring to achieve economic transformation and diversification.

. To share best practices and lessons learned from Qatar's experience in navigating the complexities of economic transformation.

Conclusion

By documenting and analyzing Qatar's path to economic self-sufficiency and diversification, this book aims to provide valuable insights and practical knowledge for policymakers, researchers, economists, and anyone interested in economic development. It seeks to contribute to the global discourse on economic diversification and transformation, highlighting Qatar as a model of strategic vision and innovation.

CHAPTER 2: HISTORICAL CONTEXT

Economic Foundations of Qatar

The economic foundations of Qatar are deeply rooted in its geographic location, natural resources, and historical trading activities. Before the discovery of oil, Qatar's economy was modest and centered around a few key activities that sustained the livelihoods of its people. Understanding these foundations is crucial to appreciating the transformation that has taken place over the past century.

Pre-Oil Economy

Pearling Industry

- **Mainstay of the Economy**: Before oil, the pearling industry was the cornerstone of Qatar's economy. The warm, shallow waters of the Arabian Gulf were ideal for pearl diving, which became the primary source of income for many Qatari families.

- **Economic Significance**: Pearls from Qatar were highly valued and traded across the region and beyond, reaching markets in India, Persia, and even Europe. This trade brought wealth and prosperity to the local population.

- **Social Structure**: The pearling industry shaped the social and economic structures of Qatar. Many communities were built around pearling activities, with entire families and tribes involved in diving, trading, and processing pearls.

Fishing and Maritime Trade

- **Supplementary Income**: Fishing was another significant activity that supplemented the income of those involved in pearling. The abundant marine life in the Gulf provided a steady source of food and trade goods.

- **Trade Routes**: Qatar's strategic location along the Arabian Gulf facilitated maritime trade. Dhows (traditional wooden boats) were used for trading goods such as dates, fish, and other local products with neighboring regions, including Bahrain, Kuwait, and the Arabian Peninsula.

Agriculture and Livestock

- **Limited Agriculture**: Due to its arid climate and scarce water resources, Qatar had limited agricultural activities. Date palm cultivation was one of the few viable agricultural practices, providing a staple food and trade commodity.

- **Livestock Rearing**: The nomadic Bedouin communities of Qatar also engaged in livestock rearing, particularly goats and camels, which were essential for transportation, milk, meat, and trade.

The Oil Boom and Its Impact

Discovery of Oil

- **Turning Point**: The discovery of oil in the 1930s and the beginning of its commercial production in the 1940s marked a turning point in Qatar's economic history. The first oil fields were developed in Dukhan, on the western coast of Qatar.

- **Foreign Investment**: The oil industry attracted significant foreign investment, primarily from British and American companies, which provided the necessary capital and expertise for exploration and production.

Economic Transformation

- **Revenue Generation**: Oil revenues transformed Qatar's economy, providing the financial resources needed for infrastructure development, modernization, and social welfare programs.

- **Urbanization**: The influx of wealth from oil led to rapid urbanization, particularly in Doha, the capital city. Modern buildings, roads, and public services were developed, changing the landscape of the country.

- **Population Growth**: The oil industry attracted workers from various parts of the world, leading to a significant increase in Qatar's population. This diverse workforce brought new skills and contributed to the country's economic growth.

Modernization and Development

- **Infrastructure Development**: Oil wealth funded extensive infrastructure projects, including ports, airports, roads, schools, hospitals, and housing. This laid the foundation for Qatar's future economic diversification.

- **Social Services**: The government invested in social services, providing free education, healthcare, and housing to its citizens. These improvements significantly enhanced the quality of life and human capital in Qatar.

- **Economic Diversification**: Recognizing the finite nature of oil resources, Qatar began to invest in diversifying its economy. This included developing the natural gas sector, petrochemicals, and other non-oil industries.

Strategic Investments

- **Sovereign Wealth Fund**: The Qatar Investment Authority (QIA) was established in 2005 to manage the country's oil and gas surpluses. The QIA invests in a diversified portfolio of global assets, ensuring long-term financial stability and reducing dependency on hydrocarbon revenues.

- **Global Investments**: Qatar has made strategic investments in various sectors worldwide, including real estate, banking, technology, and sports. These investments have not only diversified income sources but also increased Qatar's global influence.

Socio-Economic Changes

- **Improved Living Standards**: The wealth generated from oil significantly improved the living standards of Qatari citizens, with higher incomes, better housing, and access to modern amenities.

- **Education and Health**: Substantial investments were made in education and healthcare, resulting in higher literacy rates, better health outcomes, and the development of a skilled workforce.

- **Cultural Preservation**: Alongside modernization, Qatar has invested in preserving its cultural heritage. This includes the promotion of traditional crafts, music, and the establishment of cultural institutions like the Museum of Islamic Art.

Diversification of the Economy

Natural Gas Industry

- **LNG Exporter**: Qatar has become one of the world's leading exporters of liquefied natural gas (LNG), with the North Field being one of the largest gas reserves globally. This has significantly contributed to the country's GDP and government revenues.

- **Energy Security**: By investing in natural gas, Qatar has ensured a steady revenue stream while positioning itself as a key player in the global energy market.

Petrochemicals and Manufacturing

- **Value Addition**: Developing the petrochemical sector has allowed Qatar to add value to its hydrocarbon resources. Facilities like the Qatar Petrochemical Company (QAPCO) produce a wide range of chemical products.

- **Industrial Growth**: The establishment of industrial zones, such as Ras Laffan Industrial City, has supported the growth of manufacturing and other non-oil industries, contributing to economic diversification.

Financial Sector

- **Banking and Finance**: The development of the Qatar Financial Centre (QFC) and the Qatar Stock Exchange has transformed Doha into a regional financial hub. These institutions attract international businesses and investments, further diversifying the economy.

- **Islamic Finance**: Qatar has also become a prominent center for Islamic finance, with several banks and financial institutions offering Sharia-compliant products and services.

Tourism and Hospitality

- **Global Events**: Hosting major international events, such as the FIFA World Cup 2022, has put Qatar on the global tourism map. Investments in hotels, resorts, and cultural attractions aim to boost tourism revenue.

- **Cultural Tourism**: Qatar has invested in cultural heritage sites and museums, such as the National Museum of Qatar and the Museum of Islamic Art, to attract tourists interested in the region's history and culture.

Education and Research

- **Knowledge Economy**: Qatar's investment in education and research institutions, like Qatar Foundation and Qatar University, supports the development of a knowledge-based economy. These institutions foster innovation and provide a skilled workforce.

- **Research and Development**: Establishing research centers, such as the Qatar Science and Technology Park, has promoted scientific research and technological innovation, contributing to economic diversification.

Infrastructure and Urban Development

- **Modern Cities**: The development of modern infrastructure, including the Hamad International Airport, the Doha Metro, and new urban districts like Lusail City, has enhanced Qatar's global connectivity and urban living standards.
- **Sustainability Initiatives**: Qatar is incorporating sustainability into its urban development projects, aiming to create smart, eco-friendly cities that reduce environmental impact.

Conclusion

The economic foundations of Qatar were built on pearling, fishing, and trade, providing a modest yet vital base for its early economy. The discovery of oil brought transformative change, catapulting Qatar into an era of unprecedented wealth and development. By leveraging its historical strengths and newfound wealth, Qatar has diversified its economy, investing in natural gas, petrochemicals, finance, tourism, education, and infrastructure. These strategic investments and developments have laid a robust foundation for Qatar's future economic stability and growth, making it well-positioned to navigate the challenges and opportunities of the 21st century.

Pre-oil Economy

Before the discovery of oil, Qatar's economy was modest, primarily based on natural resources and trading activities. The harsh climate and arid landscape limited agricultural activities, but the strategic location along the Arabian Gulf facilitated trade and maritime activities. Understanding the pre-oil economy provides valuable insight into the transformation and diversification efforts that followed the oil boom.

Pearling Industry

- **Mainstay of the Economy**: The pearling industry was the cornerstone of Qatar's economy before the discovery of oil. The warm, shallow waters of the Arabian Gulf were ideal for pearl diving, making Qatar one of the key players in the global pearling trade.

- **Economic Significance**: Pearls were highly valued and traded extensively, reaching markets as far as India, Persia, and Europe. This trade brought significant wealth and prosperity to the local population, allowing for the import of essential goods not available locally.

- **Social Structure**: The pearling industry influenced the social and economic structures of Qatari society. Many communities were centered around pearling activities, with entire families and tribes involved in the process. The industry provided employment for a large portion of the population, including divers, boat owners, and merchants.

Fishing and Maritime Trade

- **Supplementary Income**: Fishing was another significant activity that supplemented the income of those involved in pearling. The abundant marine life in the Gulf provided a steady source of food and trade goods.

- **Trade Routes**: Qatar's strategic location along the Arabian Gulf facilitated maritime trade. Dhows (traditional wooden boats) were used for trading goods such as dates, fish, and other local products with neighboring regions, including Bahrain, Kuwait, and the Arabian Peninsula.

- **Cultural Impact**: Maritime activities shaped the cultural identity of Qatar. The construction of dhows and the skills associated with navigation and trade were passed down through generations, becoming an integral part of

Qatari heritage.

Agriculture and Livestock

- **Limited Agriculture**: Due to its arid climate and scarce water resources, Qatar had limited agricultural activities. Date palm cultivation was one of the few viable agricultural practices, providing a staple food and trade commodity.

- **Date Palm Cultivation**: Dates were a crucial part of the diet and an important trade item. Date palm groves were cultivated in areas where water was available, and the fruits were traded locally and regionally.

- **Livestock Rearing**: The nomadic Bedouin communities of Qatar also engaged in livestock rearing, particularly goats and camels. These animals were essential for transportation, milk, meat, and trade. Camels, in particular, were valued for their endurance and ability to travel long distances in the desert.

Social and Economic Structures

- **Tribal System**: The social structure in pre-oil Qatar was based on tribal affiliations. Tribes provided social cohesion and security, with each tribe having its own leaders and territories. This tribal system played a crucial role in organizing economic activities and trade.

- **Subsistence Living**: The economy was primarily subsistence-based, with people relying on local resources for their daily needs. The harsh environment required resilience and adaptability, traits that became ingrained in Qatari culture.

- **Trade Networks**: Qatar's location on the trade routes of the Arabian Gulf allowed it to become a hub for regional trade. Goods such as textiles, spices, and metals were exchanged, and Qataris developed strong trading relationships with their neighbors.

Economic Challenges

. **Environmental Constraints**: The arid climate and lack of freshwater resources limited agricultural production and posed challenges for sustaining large populations.

. **Economic Vulnerability**: The pre-oil economy was vulnerable to external factors, such as fluctuations in pearl prices and competition from other pearling regions. Natural disasters, such as storms, could also impact fishing and pearling activities.

Cultural and Economic Resilience

. **Adaptation and Innovation**: Despite the challenges, Qataris demonstrated remarkable resilience and adaptability. They developed innovative techniques for pearl diving and fishing, and their expertise in maritime trade allowed them to navigate and thrive in a harsh environment.

. **Cultural Identity**: The pre-oil economy and associated activities deeply influenced Qatar's cultural identity. Traditions related to pearling, fishing, and trading became integral parts of Qatari heritage, celebrated in festivals and preserved in museums.

Transition to the Oil Era

. **Economic Transformation**: The discovery of oil in the 1930s and the beginning of its commercial production in the 1940s marked a significant turning point. The oil industry brought unprecedented wealth and development, transforming Qatar from a modest trading outpost into a prosperous modern state.

. **Social Impact**: The newfound oil wealth led to rapid urbanization, modernization, and improvements in living standards. However, the transition also required significant adjustments as traditional economic activities gave way to new industries.

Conclusion

The pre-oil economy of Qatar, based on pearling, fishing, and limited agriculture, laid the foundations for the nation's development. The skills, resilience, and cultural heritage developed during this period provided a strong base for the rapid transformation that followed the discovery of oil. Understanding this historical context is essential for appreciating the significant economic and social changes that have shaped modern Qatar.

The Oil Boom and its Impact

The discovery of oil in the 1930s and its commercial production in the 1940s marked a watershed moment in Qatar's history, fundamentally altering its economic and social landscape. This transformation set the stage for Qatar's rapid modernization and development, propelling the country from a modest, resource-constrained economy to one of the wealthiest nations per capita.

Discovery of Oil

- **Early Exploration**: The first significant discovery of oil in Qatar occurred in 1939 at the Dukhan field on the west coast of the country. This discovery was preceded by extensive geological surveys and explorations conducted by foreign oil companies, particularly those from Britain and the United States.

- **Commercial Production**: Commercial production of oil began in 1949, with the first shipment of crude oil exported the same year. This marked the beginning of Qatar's transformation into a major player in the global energy market.

Economic Transformation

- **Revenue Generation**: The export of oil generated substantial revenue, providing the financial resources needed for large-scale infrastructure development, modernization, and social welfare programs. Oil revenue quickly became the backbone of Qatar's economy, accounting for a significant portion of the country's GDP and government income.

- **Infrastructure Development**: The newfound wealth from oil allowed for rapid infrastructure development. This included the construction of modern ports, airports, roads, schools, hospitals, and housing. Doha, the capital city, underwent significant urbanization, with modern buildings and facilities replacing traditional structures.

- **Urbanization**: The influx of wealth from oil led to the rapid urbanization of Doha and other major cities. The development of modern infrastructure, including transportation networks, healthcare facilities, and educational institutions, significantly improved the quality of life for Qatari citizens.

- **Population Growth**: The booming oil industry attracted workers from various parts of the world, leading to a significant increase in Qatar's population. This diverse workforce brought new skills and contributed to the country's economic growth. The population growth necessitated further investments in infrastructure and public services.

Modernization and Development

- **Healthcare and Education**: Oil revenues enabled the government to invest heavily in healthcare and education. Modern hospitals and clinics were built, providing high-quality medical services to citizens and residents. Education systems were overhauled, with new schools and universities established to cater to the growing population and future workforce needs.

- **Social Services**: The government implemented extensive social welfare programs, providing free education, healthcare, and housing to its citizens. These initiatives significantly improved living standards and contributed to the overall well-being of the population.

- **Economic Diversification**: Recognizing the finite nature of oil resources, Qatar began to invest in diversifying its economy. This included developing the natural gas sector, petrochemicals, and other non-oil industries to ensure long-term economic stability and growth.

Strategic Investments

- **Sovereign Wealth Fund**: To manage and invest the surplus revenues generated from oil and gas, the Qatar Investment Authority (QIA) was established in 2005. The QIA invests in a diversified portfolio of global assets, including real estate, equities, and infrastructure projects, ensuring long-term financial stability and reducing dependency on hydrocarbon revenues.

- **Global Investments**: Qatar has made strategic investments in various sectors worldwide, including real estate, banking, technology, and sports. These investments not only diversify income sources but also increase Qatar's global influence and economic resilience.

Socio-Economic Changes

- **Improved Living Standards**: The wealth generated from oil significantly improved the living standards of Qatari citizens. Higher incomes, better housing, and access to modern amenities contributed to a higher quality of life.

- **Cultural Preservation**: Alongside modernization, Qatar has invested in preserving its cultural heritage. This includes the promotion of traditional crafts, music, and the establishment of cultural institutions like the Museum of Islamic Art. The government has sought to balance modernization with the preservation of Qatar's rich cultural heritage.

Environmental and Sustainability Considerations

- **Resource Management**: With the rise of the oil industry, Qatar has faced challenges related to resource management and environmental sustainability. Efforts have been made to ensure that oil extraction and production processes are conducted responsibly, minimizing environmental impact.

. **Renewable Energy Initiatives**: In response to global environmental concerns, Qatar has begun to invest in renewable energy sources, particularly solar power. These initiatives aim to diversify the energy mix and reduce the country's carbon footprint.

Long-Term Vision

. **Qatar National Vision 2030**: Launched in 2008, the Qatar National Vision 2030 (QNV 2030) outlines the country's long-term development goals, focusing on economic diversification, sustainable development, and human capital development. This vision aims to transform Qatar into an advanced society capable of sustaining its development and providing a high standard of living for its population.

. **Economic Diversification**: A key component of QNV 2030 is economic diversification. By investing in sectors such as finance, tourism, manufacturing, and technology, Qatar aims to reduce its dependency on oil and gas revenues and build a resilient and diversified economy.

Conclusion

The oil boom marked a turning point in Qatar's history, driving unprecedented economic growth and modernization. The revenues generated from oil exports fueled infrastructure development, social welfare programs, and economic diversification efforts, transforming Qatar into a prosperous and modern state. The establishment of strategic investments and the implementation of long-term development plans, such as Qatar National Vision 2030, have positioned Qatar for sustained growth and stability in the future. Understanding the impact of the oil boom is essential for appreciating the significant economic and social changes that have shaped modern Qatar and its ongoing efforts to diversify and achieve sustainable development.

CHAPTER 3: VISION 2030: THE BLUEPRINT FOR TRANSFORMATION

Overview of Qatar National Vision 2030

Qatar National Vision 2030 (QNV 2030) was launched in October 2008 as a comprehensive framework guiding the country's development across multiple dimensions. QNV 2030 outlines Qatar's aspirations to become a sustainable and diversified economy, providing a high standard of living for its citizens while preserving cultural heritage and ensuring environmental sustainability. This visionary plan reflects the leadership's commitment to transforming Qatar into an advanced society capable of sustaining its development and providing a high quality of life for its people.

Key Objectives of QNV 2030

1. **Economic Diversification**: Reduce dependency on hydrocarbon revenues by developing a diversified economy with robust non-oil sectors such as finance, tourism, manufacturing, and technology.

2. **Sustainable Development**: Achieve balanced growth that meets the needs of the present without compromising the ability of future generations to meet their own needs, encompassing economic, social, and environmental sustainability.

3. **Human Capital Development**: Invest in education, healthcare, and skills training to build a capable and motivated workforce that drives innovation and productivity.

4. **Social Cohesion**: Foster an inclusive society that promotes social justice, equal opportunities, and high standards of living for all citizens, while preserving cultural heritage and values.

Strategic Pillars of QNV 2030

QNV 2030 is structured around four interrelated pillars, each contributing to the overarching goals of sustainable and inclusive development:

1. **Economic Development**

   - **Diversification and Competitiveness**: Promote economic diversification to create a resilient economy. This involves developing sectors such as finance, tourism, manufacturing, and technology, and enhancing the business environment to attract investment and foster innovation.

   - **Infrastructure Development**: Invest in world-class infrastructure to support economic activities and improve connectivity, including transportation networks, industrial zones, and digital infrastructure.

   - **Private Sector Growth**: Encourage the growth of the private sector by creating a conducive business environment, providing financial incentives, and supporting entrepreneurship.

2. **Social Development**

   - **Justice and Equality**: Ensure a just and inclusive society with equal opportunities for all citizens, promoting social justice and reducing disparities.

   - **Cultural Identity**: Preserve and promote Qatari cultural heritage and values, fostering a sense of national identity and pride.

. **Healthcare and Education**: Provide high-quality healthcare and education services to enhance the well-being and skills of the population. This includes building state-of-the-art healthcare facilities and reforming the education system to meet future market needs.

3. **Environmental Development**

. **Sustainable Resource Management**: Use natural resources efficiently and responsibly to ensure long-term sustainability. This includes managing water resources, conserving biodiversity, and promoting sustainable agricultural practices.

. **Renewable Energy**: Invest in renewable energy sources, such as solar power, to diversify the energy mix and reduce the country's carbon footprint.

. **Environmental Protection**: Implement policies and regulations to protect the natural environment and promote biodiversity, ensuring that economic development does not come at the expense of environmental degradation.

4. **Human Development**

. **Education and Skills Training**: Reform the education system to meet the needs of a modern economy, providing quality education and vocational training to equip citizens with the skills needed for the future.

. **Empowerment of Women and Youth**: Empower women and youth to participate fully in the economy and society, providing opportunities for leadership, innovation, and entrepreneurship.

. **Health and Well-being**: Ensure access to quality healthcare services for all citizens, promoting physical and mental well-being as key components of human development.

Implementation Strategies and Milestones

To achieve the objectives of QNV 2030, Qatar has outlined several strategies and milestones, including:

1. **Regulatory Reforms**: Introduce regulatory reforms to create a more attractive investment climate, simplify business procedures, and strengthen legal frameworks to protect investments and intellectual property.

2. **Infrastructure Investments**: Develop and upgrade transportation networks, including roads, ports, and airports, and establish industrial zones and free zones to attract foreign investment and support economic activities.

3. **Public-Private Partnerships (PPPs)**: Encourage collaboration between the government and private sector to leverage resources and expertise for development projects. PPPs are crucial for financing and implementing large-scale infrastructure and social projects.

4. **Innovation and Research**: Invest in research and development to drive technological advancements and foster a culture of innovation. Establish innovation hubs, incubators, and research centers to support startups and entrepreneurs.

5. **Human Capital Development**: Enhance human capital through continuous education, skills training, and professional development programs. This includes reforming the education system, expanding vocational training, and promoting lifelong learning.

6. **Environmental Sustainability**: Implement policies and initiatives to promote environmental sustainability,

such as renewable energy projects, conservation programs, and sustainable urban planning. These efforts aim to balance economic growth with environmental protection.

Key Milestones

. **Short-term (by 2025)**: Establish foundational regulatory frameworks, invest in critical infrastructure projects, and launch initial phases of key diversification initiatives.

. **Medium-term (by 2030)**: Achieve significant progress in economic diversification, with substantial growth in non-oil sectors. Enhance human capital development through education and training reforms, and implement advanced environmental sustainability measures.

. **Long-term (beyond 2030)**: Transition towards a fully diversified and sustainable economy, with a high standard of living for all citizens. Achieve leadership in innovation, environmental stewardship, and social development on a global scale.

Challenges and Opportunities

Challenges

1. **Global Economic Volatility**: Fluctuations in global markets, particularly in the energy sector, can impact economic stability. Qatar needs to build resilience against such volatility through diversification and strategic investments.

2. **Geopolitical Risks**: The geopolitical landscape of the Middle East presents unique challenges for Qatar. Navigating these risks requires diplomatic agility and strategic foresight.

3. **Resource Constraints**: Limited natural resources and arid climate conditions pose challenges to agricultural self-sufficiency and sustainability. Innovative solutions

and efficient resource management are essential to address these constraints.

Opportunities

1. **Technological Innovation**: Leveraging advancements in technology and innovation can drive economic diversification and enhance competitiveness. Qatar has the opportunity to become a leader in fields such as fintech, renewable energy, and smart city development.

2. **Strategic Investments**: Qatar's sovereign wealth fund, the Qatar Investment Authority (QIA), provides a strong financial base for strategic investments globally. These investments can generate returns and build economic resilience.

3. **Cultural Diplomacy**: Qatar's investments in cultural and educational institutions, such as the Qatar Foundation and the Museum of Islamic Art, enhance its global influence and promote cultural diplomacy.

Conclusion

Qatar National Vision 2030 is a bold and comprehensive roadmap for the country's future, reflecting a commitment to sustainable development, economic diversification, and human capital development. By leveraging its strengths and addressing the challenges, Qatar aims to transform into a resilient, innovative, and prosperous nation. The successful implementation of QNV 2030 will ensure that Qatar continues to thrive and maintain a high standard of living for its citizens, while preserving its cultural heritage and protecting the environment for future generations.

CHAPTER 4: ECONOMIC DIVERSIFICATION STRATEGIES

Rationale for Diversification

Economic diversification is essential for Qatar to reduce its dependency on hydrocarbon revenues and ensure long-term economic stability and growth. Diversification helps mitigate the risks associated with fluctuating oil prices and global economic volatility. By developing a broad range of industries, Qatar aims to create a resilient economy capable of withstanding global market fluctuations and fostering sustainable development.

Key Sectors for Diversification

Qatar has identified several key sectors for diversification, each playing a crucial role in achieving the objectives outlined in Qatar National Vision 2030.

Finance

- **Financial Services Growth**: Developing a robust financial sector is critical for supporting other economic activities. Qatar aims to become a regional financial hub, attracting international banks, insurance companies, and investment firms.
- **Qatar Financial Centre (QFC)**: The establishment of the QFC provides a business-friendly environment with modern infrastructure, regulatory support, and tax incentives to attract financial institutions from around the world.
- **Islamic Finance**: Qatar has positioned itself as a

leader in Islamic finance, offering a range of Sharia-compliant banking and investment products. This sector has significant growth potential both regionally and globally.

Tourism

- **Global Events**: Hosting major international events, such as the FIFA World Cup 2022, has put Qatar on the global tourism map. Investments in hotels, resorts, and cultural attractions aim to boost tourism revenue and enhance Qatar's international reputation.

- **Cultural Tourism**: Qatar has invested in cultural heritage sites and museums, such as the National Museum of Qatar and the Museum of Islamic Art, to attract tourists interested in the region's history and culture.

- **Medical and Business Tourism**: Developing medical tourism by building state-of-the-art healthcare facilities and attracting patients from the region. Additionally, promoting Qatar as a destination for international conferences and business events.

Manufacturing

- **Industrial Development**: Expanding industrial production capabilities to add value to raw materials and reduce reliance on imports. This includes developing sectors such as petrochemicals, metals, and construction materials.

- **Special Economic Zones**: Establishing industrial zones and free zones, such as Ras Laffan Industrial City and the Qatar Free Zones, provides incentives for manufacturing companies to set up operations in Qatar.

- **Technology Integration**: Incorporating advanced manufacturing technologies and automation to increase efficiency and competitiveness in the global market.

Agriculture

- **Food Security**: Enhancing food security through innovative farming practices and reducing dependency on food imports. This is particularly important given Qatar's arid climate and limited arable land.

- **Innovations in Agriculture**: Investing in modern agricultural techniques such as hydroponics, vertical farming, and aquaponics to maximize productivity and sustainability.

- **Government Support**: Implementing government programs and providing incentives for private sector investments in agriculture to boost domestic food production.

Technology

- **Digital Transformation**: Investing in digital infrastructure and fostering a culture of innovation to drive economic growth. This includes developing smart cities, e-government services, and digital finance platforms.

- **Technology Ecosystem**: Establishing a vibrant technology ecosystem with startups, incubators, and research centers contributing to technological advancements and economic diversification.

- **Research and Development**: Promoting research and development in cutting-edge technologies such as artificial intelligence, blockchain, and renewable energy solutions.

Government Policies and Initiatives

The Qatari government has introduced several policies and initiatives to support economic diversification. These include financial incentives, regulatory reforms, and infrastructure development projects.

Financial Incentives

- **Tax Benefits**: Offering tax exemptions and incentives for foreign and local businesses operating in key sectors such as finance, manufacturing, and technology.
- **Investment Grants**: Providing grants and subsidies for startups and businesses investing in innovative technologies and practices.

Regulatory Reforms

- **Ease of Doing Business**: Simplifying business registration processes, reducing bureaucratic hurdles, and improving transparency to create a more attractive investment climate.
- **Legal Frameworks**: Strengthening legal frameworks to protect intellectual property, enforce contracts, and ensure fair competition.

Infrastructure Development

- **Transportation Networks**: Developing and upgrading transportation infrastructure, including roads, ports, airports, and public transportation systems such as the Doha Metro, to support economic activities.
- **Industrial Zones**: Establishing specialized economic zones and industrial parks to attract foreign direct investment and support the growth of manufacturing and technology sectors.

Case Studies of Successful Diversification Efforts

Financial Sector Growth

- **Qatar Financial Centre (QFC)**: The QFC has successfully attracted numerous international financial institutions, making Doha a regional hub for banking and finance. The QFC offers a business-friendly environment with regulatory support and tax incentives.
- **Islamic Finance**: Qatar's leadership in Islamic finance has been recognized globally, with institutions like

Qatar Islamic Bank and Qatar International Islamic Bank offering a range of Sharia-compliant products.

Tourism Development

. **FIFA World Cup 2022**: Hosting the FIFA World Cup has significantly boosted Qatar's tourism sector. Investments in infrastructure, hotels, and cultural attractions have increased the country's visibility and attractiveness as a tourist destination.

. **Cultural Tourism**: The development of cultural institutions such as the Museum of Islamic Art and the National Museum of Qatar has attracted tourists and enhanced Qatar's cultural heritage preservation.

Manufacturing and Industrial Zones

. **Ras Laffan Industrial City**: This industrial zone has become a major center for the production of liquefied natural gas (LNG) and petrochemicals, contributing significantly to Qatar's GDP and export revenues.

. **Qatar Free Zones**: These zones offer attractive incentives for businesses, including tax exemptions, 100% foreign ownership, and streamlined customs procedures. They have successfully attracted numerous international companies.

Agricultural Innovations

. **Hydroponics and Vertical Farming**: Qatar has invested in modern farming techniques to overcome the challenges posed by its arid climate. These innovations have increased domestic food production and contributed to food security.

. **Government Programs**: Initiatives such as the Qatar National Food Security Program have provided support for agricultural projects, enhancing the country's self-sufficiency in food production.

Technology and Innovation

- **Qatar Science and Technology Park (QSTP)**: QSTP serves as a hub for research and development, supporting startups and fostering innovation in sectors such as ICT, energy, environment, and health.
- **Smart Cities**: Projects like Lusail City incorporate advanced technologies to create sustainable and efficient urban environments, positioning Qatar as a leader in smart city development.

Conclusion

Qatar's economic diversification strategies are comprehensive and multi-faceted, aiming to build a resilient, sustainable, and prosperous economy. By focusing on key sectors such as finance, tourism, manufacturing, agriculture, and technology, and implementing supportive government policies and initiatives, Qatar is well-positioned to achieve its long-term goals outlined in Qatar National Vision 2030. The success stories and ongoing efforts in various sectors demonstrate the effectiveness of these strategies in reducing dependency on hydrocarbons and fostering inclusive growth. Understanding and learning from these strategies can provide valuable insights for other nations seeking to diversify their economies and achieve sustainable development.

CHAPTER 6: AGRICULTURAL SELF-SUFFICIENCY

Challenges of Food Security in Qatar

Achieving food security in Qatar is a multifaceted challenge due to various environmental, economic, geopolitical, and technological factors. The country's unique climate and geography, along with its reliance on imports, necessitates innovative solutions and strategic planning.

Environmental Challenges

1. **Arid Climate**:

   - **High Temperatures**: Qatar experiences extremely high temperatures, particularly during the summer months, often exceeding 45°C (113°F). These temperatures are not conducive to most types of traditional crop cultivation.

   - **Low Rainfall**: The country receives very low annual rainfall, averaging less than 100 mm per year. This lack of precipitation severely limits the availability of natural water resources for irrigation.

2. **Water Scarcity**:

   - **Limited Freshwater Sources**: Qatar has very limited freshwater resources. Groundwater is the primary natural source, but it is scarce and over-extracted, leading to depletion and salinity issues.

   - **Dependence on Desalination**: The country

relies heavily on desalination to meet its water needs. While desalination provides a reliable source of potable water, it is energy-intensive and expensive.

3. **Soil Salinity**:

   - **Saline Soils**: Much of Qatar's soil is saline, which inhibits plant growth and reduces agricultural productivity. High soil salinity makes it difficult to grow many types of crops without significant soil treatment and management.

Economic Challenges

1. **High Production Costs**:

   - **Energy and Water Costs**: The costs associated with energy and water for irrigation are high due to the need for desalination and the import of agricultural inputs. These costs increase the overall expense of local food production.

   - **Infrastructure Investments**: Developing advanced agricultural infrastructure, such as greenhouses, hydroponic systems, and vertical farms, requires substantial capital investment. These technologies are essential for overcoming environmental constraints but are expensive to implement and maintain.

2. **Scale and Efficiency**:

   - **Small-scale Operations**: The agricultural sector in Qatar consists mainly of small-scale operations that struggle to achieve economies of scale. This limits their ability to compete with imported food products, which are often cheaper due to large-scale production and lower costs in other countries.

. **Productivity and Yield**: Maximizing agricultural productivity and yields in a challenging environment requires continuous investment in research, technology, and skilled labor. Maintaining high productivity levels is a constant challenge.

Geopolitical Challenges

1. Reliance on Imports:

. **Import Dependency**: Qatar has historically imported around 90% of its food. This high dependency makes the country vulnerable to global supply chain disruptions, trade restrictions, and price fluctuations.

. **Trade Routes and Diplomacy**: Ensuring stable and reliable trade routes is essential for importing food. Geopolitical tensions and diplomatic relations can affect the availability and cost of imported food products.

2. Food Price Volatility:

. **Global Market Fluctuations**: The prices of imported food products are subject to global market fluctuations. Factors such as climate change, international conflicts, and economic policies in exporting countries can lead to sudden increases in food prices.

. **Economic Sanctions and Embargoes**: Qatar's food security can be affected by international sanctions or embargoes imposed on trading partners. Such geopolitical events can disrupt supply chains and lead to shortages or higher prices.

Technological and Resource Management Challenges

1. Technological Adaptation:

. **Adoption of Advanced Techniques**: While innovative agricultural technologies like hydroponics, vertical farming, and aquaponics hold promise, their adoption requires technical expertise, investment, and ongoing research.

. **Maintenance and Upkeep**: Advanced agricultural systems require regular maintenance and monitoring to ensure optimal performance. Technical failures or resource mismanagement can result in significant production losses.

2. **Resource Management**:

. **Efficient Water Use**: Managing water resources efficiently is critical in Qatar's arid environment. Techniques such as drip irrigation and recirculating water systems must be optimized to reduce waste and maximize crop yields.

. **Energy Consumption**: Desalination and advanced farming technologies consume substantial amounts of energy. Balancing energy use with sustainable practices and renewable energy sources is a significant challenge.

Sustainability and Environmental Impact

1. **Environmental Sustainability**:

. **Sustainable Practices**: Implementing sustainable agricultural practices that minimize environmental impact is essential. This includes reducing water usage, minimizing chemical inputs, and promoting biodiversity.

. **Climate Change**: Addressing the impacts of climate change, such as increased temperatures and changing precipitation patterns, is crucial for long-term agricultural sustainability.

2. Renewable Energy Integration:

. **Energy Needs**: Integrating renewable energy sources, such as solar power, into agricultural operations can help reduce the environmental footprint and improve sustainability. However, this requires investment in infrastructure and technology.

Social and Economic Resilience

1. Community Engagement:

. **Public Awareness**: Raising awareness about the importance of food security and promoting local food production can help build community support and participation in agricultural initiatives.

. **Education and Training**: Providing education and training programs for farmers and agribusinesses is essential for building a skilled workforce capable of implementing advanced agricultural techniques.

2. Economic Resilience:

. **Diversification**: Diversifying the agricultural sector and promoting value-added products can enhance economic resilience and reduce dependency on imports.

. **Investment in Research**: Ongoing investment in agricultural research and development is crucial for addressing the unique challenges faced by Qatar's agricultural sector and finding innovative solutions.

Conclusion

Achieving food security in Qatar is a multifaceted challenge that requires addressing environmental, economic, geopolitical, and technological factors. By embracing innovative agricultural practices, investing in research and development, and fostering public-private partnerships, Qatar can enhance its food production capabilities and reduce dependency on imports. The government's proactive policies and support for sustainable agriculture are essential in overcoming these challenges and ensuring long-term food security for the nation.

CHAPTER 7: TECHNOLOGY AND INNOVATION

Role of Technology in Economic Transformation

Technology is a critical driver of economic transformation, enabling innovation, efficiency, and competitiveness. For Qatar, leveraging technology and fostering innovation are essential for achieving the objectives outlined in Qatar National Vision 2030. This chapter explores the role of technology in Qatar's economic diversification, the development of its technology ecosystem, and case studies of successful technological innovations.

Key Areas of Technological Focus

1. **Digital Transformation**:
   - **Smart Cities**: Qatar is investing in the development of smart cities, such as Lusail City, which integrate digital technologies to enhance urban living. Smart city initiatives include intelligent transportation systems, smart grids, and digital public services.
   - **E-Government Services**: The government is enhancing public service delivery through e-government platforms, making services more accessible and efficient for citizens and businesses.

2. **Information and Communication Technology (ICT)**:
   - **Broadband Infrastructure**: Expanding high-speed internet connectivity across the

country to support digital transformation and innovation.

- **Cybersecurity**: Strengthening cybersecurity measures to protect critical infrastructure, businesses, and citizens from digital threats.

3. **Research and Development (R&D)**:

- **Innovation Hubs**: Establishing innovation hubs and research centers, such as Qatar Science and Technology Park (QSTP), to foster research and development in various fields.

- **Collaboration with Universities**: Partnering with leading universities and research institutions to advance scientific research and technological innovation.

4. **Advanced Manufacturing**:

- **Industry 4.0**: Adopting Industry 4.0 technologies, including automation, artificial intelligence (AI), and the Internet of Things (IoT), to enhance manufacturing efficiency and competitiveness.

- **3D Printing**: Utilizing 3D printing technology for rapid prototyping and manufacturing of complex components.

Qatar's Technology Ecosystem

Qatar has established a vibrant technology ecosystem with numerous startups, incubators, and research centers contributing to technological advancements and economic diversification.

Qatar Science and Technology Park (QSTP)

- **Innovation Hub**: QSTP is a leading hub for technology development and innovation, providing a supportive environment for startups and established companies. It offers state-of-the-art facilities, funding opportunities, and access to a network of industry experts.

. **Research and Collaboration**: QSTP collaborates with local and international universities, research institutions, and businesses to drive research and development in key areas such as ICT, energy, environment, and health.

Incubators and Accelerators

. **Support for Startups**: Qatar has several incubators and accelerators that support the growth of startups by providing mentorship, funding, and access to resources. Examples include the Digital Incubation Center (DIC) and Qatar Business Incubation Center (QBIC).

. **Startup Ecosystem**: The startup ecosystem in Qatar is vibrant, with numerous tech startups emerging in fields such as fintech, Healthtech, edtech, and e-commerce.

Research Institutions

. **Qatar Foundation**: Qatar Foundation supports a range of research institutions and initiatives aimed at advancing scientific research and technological innovation. It includes entities such as the Qatar Biomedical Research Institute (QBRI) and the Qatar Computing Research Institute (QCRI).

. **Education City**: Education City hosts campuses of several international universities, fostering a collaborative environment for research and innovation in various disciplines.

Public-Private Partnerships

. **Collaboration for Innovation**: Public-private partnerships (PPPs) play a crucial role in driving technological innovation in Qatar. These collaborations bring together government entities, private companies, and research institutions to work on projects that address national priorities and challenges.

Case Studies of Technological Innovations

Fintech

- **Qatar Fintech Hub**: The Qatar Fintech Hub (QFTH) is an initiative to support the development of fintech startups and solutions. It provides mentorship, funding, and access to a global network of financial institutions.
- **Digital Payment Solutions**: Several fintech startups in Qatar are developing digital payment solutions, enhancing financial inclusion and transforming the financial services sector.

Healthcare Technology

- **Sidra Medicine**: Sidra Medicine is a state-of-the-art medical and research facility that leverages advanced technologies for patient care and medical research. It focuses on precision medicine, genomics, and biomedical research.
- **Telemedicine**: The adoption of telemedicine platforms has increased, providing remote healthcare services and consultations, especially during the COVID-19 pandemic.

Renewable Energy

- **Solar Power Projects**: Qatar is investing in solar power projects to diversify its energy mix and promote sustainability. The Al Kharsaah Solar PV Power Plant is a significant project aimed at increasing the country's renewable energy capacity.
- **Energy Research**: Research institutions like the Qatar Environment and Energy Research Institute (QEERI) are conducting studies on renewable energy technologies and sustainable energy solutions.

Smart Cities

- **Lusail City**: Lusail City is a pioneering smart city project that integrates advanced technologies to enhance urban living. It features smart infrastructure, intelligent transportation systems, and sustainable building practices.
- **Digital Twins**: The use of digital twin technology in urban planning and infrastructure management allows for real-time monitoring and optimization of city operations.

Artificial Intelligence (AI)

- **AI Research and Applications**: Qatar is investing in AI research and its applications across various sectors, including healthcare, education, and transportation. AI technologies are being used for data analysis, predictive modeling, and automation.
- **Qatar Center for Artificial Intelligence (QCAI)**: The QCAI focuses on advancing AI research and developing AI-driven solutions to address national challenges.

Environmental Sustainability

- **Smart Agriculture**: Utilizing IoT and AI technologies in agriculture to optimize resource use, monitor crop health, and increase productivity. Smart agriculture initiatives contribute to food security and sustainable farming practices.
- **Green Building Technologies**: Promoting the use of green building technologies and sustainable construction practices to reduce environmental impact and enhance energy efficiency.

Future Prospects and Goals

Qatar's commitment to technology and innovation is evident in its strategic investments and proactive policies. Looking ahead, Qatar aims to:

1. **Enhance Research and Development**: Continue

investing in R&D to drive innovation and technological advancements in key sectors.

2. **Promote Digital Transformation**: Expand digital infrastructure and promote the adoption of digital technologies across all sectors of the economy.

3. **Foster a Startup Ecosystem**: Strengthen support for startups and entrepreneurs by providing funding, mentorship, and access to markets.

4. **Develop Human Capital**: Invest in education and training programs to build a skilled workforce capable of leveraging advanced technologies.

5. **Achieve Sustainability**: Integrate sustainable practices and technologies to promote environmental sustainability and reduce the carbon footprint.

Conclusion

Technology and innovation are critical enablers of Qatar's economic transformation and diversification. By leveraging advanced technologies, fostering a vibrant innovation ecosystem, and investing in research and development, Qatar is well-positioned to achieve its long-term goals outlined in Qatar National Vision 2030. The country's commitment to embracing technology and innovation will drive economic growth, enhance competitiveness, and ensure a sustainable and prosperous future for its citizens.

CHAPTER 8: HUMAN CAPITAL DEVELOPMENT

Importance of Human Capital Development

Human capital development is essential for Qatar's economic transformation and diversification. Investing in education, healthcare, and skills training builds a capable and motivated workforce that drives innovation, productivity, and sustainable growth. This chapter explores Qatar's strategies and initiatives in human capital development, focusing on education reforms, skills training, empowerment of women and youth, and attracting and retaining talent.

Key Areas of Focus

1. **Education Reforms and Skills Training**:

   - **Quality Education**: Ensuring access to high-quality education for all citizens is a cornerstone of Qatar's human capital development strategy. This includes reforming the education system to meet the needs of a modern economy.

   - **Skills Training**: Developing vocational and technical training programs that equip individuals with the skills required in various industries, particularly those identified for economic diversification.

2. **Empowerment of Women and Youth**:

   - **Gender Equality**: Promoting gender equality and empowering women to participate fully in the economy and society.

- **Youth Engagement**: Providing opportunities for youth to develop their talents, gain skills, and take on leadership roles in various sectors.

3. **Attracting and Retaining Talent**:

- **Talent Attraction**: Creating a conducive environment to attract international talent that can contribute to Qatar's economic goals.
- **Talent Retention**: Implementing policies and programs to retain skilled professionals and prevent brain drain.

Education Reforms

Primary and Secondary Education

- **Curriculum Development**: Reforming curricula to emphasize critical thinking, creativity, and problem-solving skills. Incorporating STEM (Science, Technology, Engineering, and Mathematics) education to prepare students for future job markets.

- **Teacher Training**: Investing in teacher training and professional development to ensure high-quality instruction. Attracting and retaining skilled educators through competitive salaries and benefits.

- **Inclusive Education**: Promoting inclusive education to ensure that all children, including those with special needs, have access to quality education.

Higher Education

- **University Partnerships**: Establishing partnerships with leading international universities to provide world-class education and foster research collaboration. Examples include Education City, which hosts branches of renowned universities such as Georgetown, Northwestern, and Carnegie Mellon.

- **Research and Innovation**: Encouraging higher education institutions to focus on research and innovation. Providing funding and resources to support research initiatives that address national priorities and global challenges.

. **Scholarships and Financial Aid**: Offering scholarships and financial aid to ensure that talented students from all backgrounds can access higher education.

Technical and Vocational Education and Training (TVET)

. **Industry Collaboration**: Collaborating with industries to design and implement TVET programs that align with market needs. Ensuring that training programs are relevant and up to date with industry standards.

. **Certification and Accreditation**: Establishing certification and accreditation frameworks to ensure the quality and recognition of TVET programs. Providing pathways for lifelong learning and career advancement.

. **Apprenticeships and Internships**: Promoting apprenticeships and internships to provide hands-on experience and bridge the gap between education and employment.

Empowerment of Women and Youth

Women's Empowerment

. **Policy Support**: Implementing policies that promote gender equality and create opportunities for women in the workforce. Ensuring equal pay and career advancement opportunities.

. **Leadership Development**: Providing leadership training and mentoring programs to prepare women for leadership roles in various sectors. Encouraging female participation in decision-making processes.

. **Work-Life Balance**: Supporting work-life balance initiatives, such as flexible working hours and parental leave, to enable women to balance professional and personal responsibilities.

Youth Engagement

- **Education and Skills Development**: Investing in education and skills development programs tailored to the needs and aspirations of youth. Promoting STEM education and entrepreneurship among young people.

- **Youth Councils and Forums**: Establishing youth councils and forums to give young people a platform to voice their opinions and contribute to policymaking. Encouraging youth participation in community development projects.

- **Entrepreneurship Support**: Providing support for young entrepreneurs through funding, mentorship, and access to resources. Creating startup incubators and accelerators to nurture innovative ideas.

Attracting and Retaining Talent

Talent Attraction

- **Global Recruitment**: Developing strategies to attract international talent, including professionals, researchers, and academics. Offering competitive salaries, benefits, and opportunities for career growth.

- **International Collaboration**: Building partnerships with international organizations, universities, and research institutions to attract talent and foster knowledge exchange.

Talent Retention

- **Professional Development**: Offering continuous professional development opportunities to keep professionals engaged and updated with the latest industry trends. Providing pathways for career progression and leadership development.

- **Quality of Life**: Ensuring a high quality of life for residents through excellent healthcare, education, and recreational facilities. Promoting a safe and inclusive society that values diversity and innovation.

- **Work Environment**: Creating a supportive and dynamic work environment that encourages creativity, collaboration, and innovation. Recognizing and rewarding contributions and achievements.

Case Studies of Human Capital Development Initiatives

Qatar Foundation

- **Education City**: Qatar Foundation's Education City is a hub for higher education and research, hosting branches of prestigious international universities. It provides world-class education and fosters research collaboration across various disciplines.
- **Qatar National Research Fund (QNRF)**: QNRF funds research projects that address national priorities and contribute to the global knowledge economy. It supports researchers and promotes a culture of innovation.

Qatar Leadership Centre (QLC)

- **Leadership Programs**: QLC offers leadership development programs for young professionals, executives, and public sector leaders. These programs aim to build leadership capacity and prepare individuals for senior roles in various sectors.
- **Mentoring and Coaching**: Providing mentoring and coaching to support personal and professional growth. Encouraging leaders to develop their skills and contribute to Qatar's development.

Qatar University

- **Research Excellence**: Qatar University is committed to research excellence, focusing on areas such as energy, environment, health, and technology. It collaborates with industry partners to address national and global challenges.

- **Student Development**: Offering a range of programs and activities to support student development, including internships, career services, and extracurricular activities. Promoting a holistic approach to education that nurtures both academic and personal growth.

Future Prospects and Goals

Qatar's commitment to human capital development is evident in its strategic investments and proactive policies. Looking ahead, Qatar aims to:

1. **Enhance Education Quality**: Continuously improve the quality of education at all levels, ensuring that it meets international standards and prepares students for future challenges.

2. **Promote Lifelong Learning**: Foster a culture of lifelong learning, encouraging individuals to continuously update their skills and knowledge throughout their careers.

3. **Support Innovation and Research**: Invest in innovation and research to drive technological advancements and address national priorities. Encourage collaboration between academia, industry, and government.

4. **Empower All Citizens**: Ensure that all citizens, regardless of gender, age, or background, have access to opportunities for personal and professional growth. Promote inclusivity and diversity in all sectors.

5. **Develop a Skilled Workforce**: Build a highly skilled and adaptable workforce capable of driving economic diversification and sustainable development. Provide training and support to align workforce skills with market needs.

Conclusion

Human capital development is a cornerstone of Qatar's economic transformation and diversification. By investing in education, empowering women and youth, and attracting and retaining talent, Qatar is building a capable and motivated workforce that drives innovation and productivity. The country's commitment to human capital development will ensure a sustainable and prosperous future, aligned with the goals of Qatar National Vision 2030.

CHAPTER 9: SUSTAINABILITY AND ENVIRONMENTAL STEWARDSHIP

Integrating Sustainability into Economic Planning

Qatar's rapid economic growth has brought about significant environmental challenges. Recognizing the importance of sustainability, Qatar has integrated environmental considerations into its economic planning. This chapter explores Qatar's strategies and initiatives for promoting sustainability and environmental stewardship, focusing on renewable energy, resource management, and environmental policies.

Key Areas of Focus

1. **Sustainable Development Goals (SDGs):**

   - **Alignment with Global Goals**: Qatar is committed to achieving the United Nations Sustainable Development Goals (SDGs) by incorporating them into national policies and development plans.

   - **National Priorities**: Identifying and addressing national priorities that align with global sustainability goals, such as clean energy, sustainable cities, and climate action.

2. **Renewable Energy:**

   - **Diversifying Energy Sources**: Reducing dependency on hydrocarbons by investing in renewable energy sources like solar and wind power.

. **Energy Efficiency**: Promoting energy efficiency across all sectors to reduce consumption and emissions.

3. **Resource Management**:

. **Water Management**: Implementing efficient water management practices to address scarcity and ensure sustainable use of water resources.

. **Waste Management**: Developing comprehensive waste management systems to minimize environmental impact and promote recycling and waste-to-energy initiatives.

4. **Environmental Policies and Regulations**:

. **Policy Frameworks**: Establishing robust environmental policies and regulatory frameworks to protect natural resources and promote sustainable practices.

. **Environmental Impact Assessments (EIAs)**: Mandating EIAs for all major development projects to assess and mitigate environmental impacts.

Renewable Energy Initiatives

Solar Power

. **Al Kharsaah Solar PV Power Plant**: The Al Kharsaah Solar PV Power Plant is one of Qatar's flagship renewable energy projects. This large-scale solar farm aims to significantly increase the country's solar energy capacity and reduce reliance on fossil fuels.

. **Solar Energy Research**: Qatar is investing in research and development to advance solar energy technologies and improve efficiency. Institutions like the Qatar

Environment and Energy Research Institute (QEERI) play a crucial role in this effort.

Wind Power

- **Feasibility Studies**: Conducting feasibility studies to identify potential sites for wind power generation. These studies assess wind patterns, environmental impact, and economic viability.

- **Pilot Projects**: Implementing pilot wind power projects to gather data and evaluate the performance of wind turbines in Qatar's climate.

Energy Efficiency Programs

- **Building Standards**: Introducing energy-efficient building standards and regulations to reduce energy consumption in residential, commercial, and industrial buildings.

- **Public Awareness Campaigns**: Running public awareness campaigns to promote energy-saving practices among residents and businesses.

Resource Management Strategies

Water Management

- **Desalination**: Investing in advanced desalination technologies to provide a reliable source of potable water. Qatar is also exploring more energy-efficient and environmentally friendly desalination methods.

- **Water Conservation**: Implementing water conservation programs to reduce wastage and promote efficient use of water in agriculture, industry, and households.

- **Treated Sewage Effluent (TSE)**: Utilizing TSE for irrigation and industrial purposes to reduce the demand for freshwater.

Waste Management

- **Recycling Programs**: Establishing comprehensive recycling programs to divert waste from landfills and promote the circular economy. These programs include the collection, sorting, and processing of recyclable materials.
- **Waste-to-Energy**: Developing waste-to-energy facilities that convert non-recyclable waste into energy. This approach reduces landfill usage and provides a renewable energy source.
- **Public Education**: Educating the public about the importance of waste reduction, recycling, and proper waste disposal through campaigns and school programs.

Sustainable Agriculture

- **Innovative Farming Techniques**: Promoting the use of hydroponics, vertical farming, and aquaponics to increase agricultural productivity while conserving water and reducing environmental impact.
- **Organic Farming**: Encouraging organic farming practices to reduce the use of synthetic fertilizers and pesticides, thus protecting soil health and biodiversity.

Environmental Policies and Regulations

Policy Frameworks

- **Qatar National Environment Strategy (QNES)**: The QNES outlines Qatar's strategic approach to environmental protection and sustainable development. It sets clear objectives and targets for reducing environmental impact and promoting sustainability.
- **Regulatory Bodies**: Establishing regulatory bodies, such as the Ministry of Municipality and Environment (MME), to oversee the implementation and enforcement of environmental policies and regulations.

Environmental Impact Assessments (EIAs)

- **Mandatory Assessments**: Requiring EIAs for all major development projects to evaluate potential environmental impacts and identify mitigation measures.
- **Stakeholder Involvement**: Ensuring that stakeholders, including local communities, are involved in the EIA process to address concerns and incorporate local knowledge.

Climate Action

- **National Climate Change Action Plan**: Developing and implementing a comprehensive action plan to address climate change. This includes measures to reduce greenhouse gas emissions, enhance climate resilience, and promote sustainable practices.
- **International Collaboration**: Participating in international climate agreements and collaborating with other countries to share knowledge, technologies, and best practices for addressing climate change.

Biodiversity Conservation

- **Protected Areas**: Designating and managing protected areas to conserve Qatar's unique biodiversity. This includes marine reserves, wildlife sanctuaries, and natural parks.
- **Habitat Restoration**: Implementing habitat restoration projects to rehabilitate degraded ecosystems and promote biodiversity.
- **Species Protection**: Enforcing laws and regulations to protect endangered species and combat illegal wildlife trade.

Case Studies of Sustainability Initiatives

Qatar Green Building Council (QGBC)

- **Green Building Standards**: QGBC promotes green building practices through certification programs, guidelines, and training. It encourages the construction of energy-efficient and environmentally friendly buildings.

. **Sustainability Awards**: Recognizing and rewarding projects and organizations that demonstrate outstanding commitment to sustainability through the Qatar Sustainability Awards.

The Pearl-Qatar

. **Sustainable Urban Development**: The Pearl-Qatar is a prime example of sustainable urban development. The island features energy-efficient buildings, green spaces, and sustainable transportation options.

. **Water Management**: Implementing advanced water management systems, including greywater recycling and efficient irrigation, to minimize water usage.

National Food Security Program

. **Sustainable Agriculture**: The National Food Security Program focuses on increasing domestic food production through sustainable agricultural practices. It promotes the use of innovative farming techniques and efficient resource management.

. **Local Food Production**: Supporting local farmers and agribusinesses to enhance food security and reduce dependency on imports.

Future Prospects and Goals

Qatar's commitment to sustainability and environmental stewardship is evident in its strategic initiatives and proactive policies. Looking ahead, Qatar aims to:

1. **Expand Renewable Energy**: Continue investing in renewable energy projects, with a focus on solar and wind power, to diversify the energy mix and reduce greenhouse gas emissions.

2. **Enhance Resource Efficiency**: Implement advanced

technologies and practices to enhance resource efficiency, particularly in water and energy use.

3. **Strengthen Environmental Policies**: Further develop and enforce environmental policies and regulations to protect natural resources and promote sustainable practices.

4. **Promote Public Engagement**: Foster a culture of sustainability by engaging the public in environmental initiatives and promoting sustainable lifestyles.

5. **Achieve Climate Resilience**: Enhance climate resilience by implementing measures to adapt to the impacts of climate change and reduce vulnerability.

Conclusion

Sustainability and environmental stewardship are integral to Qatar's long-term development and economic diversification. By investing in renewable energy, efficient resource management, and robust environmental policies, Qatar is paving the way for a sustainable future. The country's commitment to sustainability will ensure that economic growth is achieved in harmony with environmental protection and social well-being, in line with the goals of Qatar National Vision 2030.

CHAPTER 10: TRADE AND INVESTMENT

Enhancing Trade Relations

Qatar's strategic location at the crossroads of major trade routes, coupled with its robust economic policies, positions it as a significant player in global trade. Enhancing trade relations is vital for diversifying the economy and reducing dependency on hydrocarbon exports. This chapter explores Qatar's strategies to strengthen trade relations, attract foreign direct investment, and develop free zones and economic zones.

Key Areas of Focus

1. **Diversification of Export Markets**:
    - **Expanding Non-Hydrocarbon Exports**: Focusing on increasing the export of non-hydrocarbon products such as petrochemicals, aluminum, fertilizers, and food products.
    - **Targeting Emerging Markets**: Strengthening trade relations with emerging markets in Asia, Africa, and Latin America to diversify export destinations.

2. **Trade Agreements and Partnerships**:
    - **Bilateral and Multilateral Agreements**: Engaging in bilateral and multilateral trade agreements to facilitate market access and reduce trade barriers.
    - **Regional Cooperation**: Enhancing cooperation with regional organizations such as the Gulf Cooperation Council (GCC) and the Arab League

to promote intra-regional trade.

3. Trade Infrastructure Development:

- **Port Facilities**: Upgrading and expanding port facilities to enhance capacity and efficiency in handling cargo.

- **Logistics and Transportation**: Developing advanced logistics and transportation networks to support seamless trade operations.

Attracting Foreign Direct Investment

Foreign direct investment (FDI) is a critical component of Qatar's economic diversification strategy. Attracting FDI brings capital, technology, and expertise that drive growth and innovation in various sectors.

Investment Incentives

- **Tax Exemptions**: Offering tax exemptions and incentives for foreign investors, including exemptions from corporate income tax for specific periods.

- **Full Foreign Ownership**: Allowing 100% foreign ownership in many sectors to attract international businesses and investors.

- **Profit Repatriation**: Permitting the repatriation of profits and capital to ensure that foreign investors can transfer their earnings back to their home countries.

Regulatory Reforms

- **Simplified Business Procedures**: Streamlining business registration and licensing procedures to make it easier for foreign investors to establish and operate businesses in Qatar.

- **Legal Frameworks**: Strengthening legal frameworks to protect intellectual property rights, enforce contracts, and ensure fair competition.

Investment Promotion

- **Qatar Investment Promotion Agency (IPA Qatar)**:

IPA Qatar plays a pivotal role in attracting FDI by promoting investment opportunities and providing support services to foreign investors.

. **Investment Roadshows and Forums**: Organizing international roadshows and investment forums to showcase Qatar's business environment and investment opportunities.

Sectoral Focus for FDI

. **Technology and Innovation**: Attracting investments in technology and innovation sectors, including ICT, fintech, and renewable energy.

. **Tourism and Hospitality**: Promoting investment in tourism infrastructure, including hotels, resorts, and cultural attractions.

. **Manufacturing and Industry**: Encouraging investment in manufacturing and industrial sectors, particularly in specialized economic zones.

Free Zones and Economic Zones

Qatar has established free zones and economic zones to create favorable conditions for businesses and attract foreign investment. These zones offer various incentives and benefits to enhance competitiveness and promote economic growth.

Qatar Free Zones Authority (QFZA)

. **QFZA Overview**: The Qatar Free Zones Authority (QFZA) oversees the development and management of free zones in Qatar, providing world-class infrastructure and business-friendly regulations.

. **Key Free Zones**: The two primary free zones managed by QFZA are Ras Bufontas and Umm Alhoul. These zones cater to different industries and offer state-of-the-art facilities and services.

Ras Bufontas Free Zone

- **Strategic Location**: Located near Hamad International Airport, Ras Bufontas Free Zone is ideal for logistics, manufacturing, and technology companies.
- **Facilities and Services**: Offering advanced facilities, including office spaces, warehouses, and light industrial units, along with support services such as customs facilitation and business consultancy.

Umm Alhoul Free Zone

- **Proximity to Hamad Port**: Situated near Hamad Port, Umm Alhoul Free Zone is designed for industries such as maritime, logistics, petrochemicals, and manufacturing.
- **Comprehensive Infrastructure**: Providing comprehensive infrastructure, including deep-water berths, industrial plots, and logistics facilities, to support diverse business activities.

Economic Zones Company (Manateq)

- **Manateq's Role**: Manateq develops and operates special economic zones, logistics parks, and warehousing complexes to attract investment and promote industrial growth.
- **Key Economic Zones**: Manateq oversees several economic zones, including the Al Karaana Industrial Zone, the Mesaieed Industrial Zone, and the Ras Bufontas Logistics Park.

Incentives and Benefits in Free Zones and Economic Zones

- **Tax and Customs Exemptions**: Offering exemptions from customs duties, corporate taxes, and personal income taxes to businesses operating in these zones.
- **Streamlined Regulations**: Providing simplified regulatory procedures and fast-track business setup processes.
- **Infrastructure and Utilities**: Ensuring access to world-

class infrastructure, utilities, and support services to facilitate business operations.

Case Studies of Successful Trade and Investment Initiatives

Hamad Port

- **World-Class Port**: Hamad Port is one of the largest and most advanced ports in the region, significantly enhancing Qatar's trade capacity.
- **Logistics Hub**: Serving as a logistics hub, Hamad Port facilitates efficient cargo handling and transshipment, connecting Qatar to global markets.

Qatar Financial Centre (QFC)

- **Financial Services Hub**: QFC has established Qatar as a regional hub for financial services, attracting international banks, insurance companies, and investment firms.
- **Business-Friendly Environment**: Offering a business-friendly environment with legal and regulatory frameworks aligned with international standards.

Qatar Science and Technology Park (QSTP)

- **Innovation Ecosystem**: QSTP is a leading hub for research and innovation, attracting technology companies, startups, and research institutions.
- **Support for R&D**: Providing support for research and development activities, including funding, facilities, and collaboration opportunities.

Future Prospects and Goals

Qatar's commitment to enhancing trade and investment is evident in its strategic initiatives and proactive policies. Looking ahead, Qatar aims to:

1. **Expand Trade Networks**: Strengthen trade networks by engaging in more bilateral and multilateral trade agreements and fostering regional cooperation.

2. **Attract High-Quality FDI**: Focus on attracting high-quality foreign direct investment in key sectors that drive economic diversification and technological innovation.

3. **Develop Competitive Free Zones**: Continue developing competitive free zones and economic zones with world-class infrastructure and business-friendly regulations.

4. **Promote Sustainable Practices**: Ensure that trade and investment activities promote sustainable development and align with environmental and social goals.

5. **Leverage Digital Transformation**: Utilize digital technologies to enhance trade operations, improve efficiency, and create new investment opportunities.

Conclusion

Trade and investment are pivotal to Qatar's economic diversification and long-term growth. By enhancing trade relations, attracting foreign direct investment, and developing free zones and economic zones, Qatar is positioning itself as a global trade and investment hub. The country's strategic initiatives and policies will ensure sustained economic growth, increased competitiveness, and a resilient economy aligned with Qatar National Vision 2030.

CHAPTER 11: CHALLENGES AND RISKS

Economic Volatility and Global Market Dynamics

Qatar's economy, like many others, is susceptible to fluctuations in global markets. Understanding and mitigating these risks are crucial for maintaining economic stability and ensuring sustainable growth.

Key Challenges

1. **Dependency on Hydrocarbons**:
   - **Price Fluctuations**: Global oil and gas prices are subject to significant volatility due to geopolitical tensions, changes in supply and demand, and economic cycles. This volatility can impact Qatar's revenue and economic planning.
   - **Diversification Efforts**: While Qatar is actively pursuing economic diversification, its current dependency on hydrocarbons means that it remains vulnerable to global energy market dynamics.

2. **Global Economic Conditions**:
   - **Recession Risks**: Global economic downturns, such as the one caused by the COVID-19 pandemic, can reduce demand for energy and other exports, negatively affecting Qatar's economy.
   - **Trade Barriers**: Protectionist policies and trade barriers imposed by other countries can hinder

Qatar's export markets and affect its economic growth.

3. **Investment Fluctuations**:

- **Foreign Direct Investment (FDI)**: Economic uncertainties can lead to fluctuations in FDI, impacting projects and economic diversification efforts.

- **Global Financial Markets**: Volatility in global financial markets can affect Qatar's investments abroad and the performance of its sovereign wealth fund, the Qatar Investment Authority (QIA).

Geopolitical Risks

Qatar's location in the Middle East presents unique geopolitical challenges that can impact its stability and economic progress.

Key Geopolitical Risks

1. **Regional Tensions**:

- **Diplomatic Disputes**: Regional disputes, such as the blockade imposed by neighboring countries in 2017, can disrupt trade, investment, and economic activities.

- **Political Instability**: Political instability in neighboring countries can spill over into Qatar, affecting its security and economic environment.

2. **Security Threats**:

- **Terrorism and Conflict**: The threat of terrorism and regional conflicts poses security risks that can impact economic activities and foreign investment.

- **Cybersecurity**: As Qatar increasingly adopts digital technologies, cybersecurity threats from state and non-state actors can jeopardize critical infrastructure and economic stability.

3. International Relations:

. **Global Alliances**: Changes in global alliances and international relations can influence Qatar's diplomatic and economic strategies.

. **Sanctions and Embargoes**: International sanctions or embargoes against key trading partners can disrupt supply chains and trade routes, impacting Qatar's economy.

Domestic Challenges

Qatar faces several domestic challenges that require strategic planning and effective policy implementation to ensure sustainable development and economic resilience.

Key Domestic Challenges

1. Infrastructure Development:

. **Urbanization**: Rapid urbanization and population growth demand continuous investment in infrastructure, such as housing, transportation, and utilities, to maintain quality of life and economic efficiency.

. **Sustainable Development**: Balancing infrastructure development with sustainability goals is essential to minimize environmental impact and ensure long-term viability.

2. Workforce and Skills Gap:

. **Labor Market Dynamics**: Qatar's labor market is characterized by a high proportion of expatriate workers. Ensuring that the local workforce has the necessary skills and opportunities is crucial for economic stability.

. **Education and Training**: Addressing the skills

gap through education and vocational training programs is essential to prepare the workforce for future economic needs and technological advancements.

3. **Regulatory and Bureaucratic Hurdles**:

   - **Ease of Doing Business**: Streamlining regulatory procedures and reducing bureaucratic hurdles are necessary to attract and retain businesses and investments.

   - **Legal Frameworks**: Strengthening legal frameworks to protect investments, intellectual property, and enforce contracts is vital for economic confidence and growth.

4. **Economic Diversification**:

   - **Implementation of Strategies**: Successfully implementing economic diversification strategies requires effective coordination among various sectors and stakeholders.

   - **Innovation and Entrepreneurship**: Fostering a culture of innovation and entrepreneurship is crucial for developing new industries and reducing dependency on hydrocarbons.

Environmental and Sustainability Risks

As Qatar aims for sustainable development, addressing environmental risks and promoting sustainability are critical to achieving long-term economic goals.

Key Environmental and Sustainability Risks

1. **Climate Change**:

   - **Rising Temperatures**: Climate change can lead to rising temperatures, which can exacerbate water scarcity and affect agriculture and public health.

   - **Sea Level Rise**: Rising sea levels pose a threat to

Qatar's coastal infrastructure and urban areas.

2. **Water Scarcity**:

. **Dependence on Desalination**: Qatar relies heavily on desalination for its water supply. Desalination is energy-intensive and has environmental impacts, making water management a significant challenge.

. **Sustainable Water Use**: Implementing sustainable water management practices is crucial to ensure long-term water security and reduce environmental impact.

3. **Environmental Degradation**:

. **Pollution**: Industrial activities, urbanization, and transportation contribute to air and water pollution, affecting public health and the environment.

. **Biodiversity Loss**: Habitat destruction and over-exploitation of natural resources threaten Qatar's biodiversity and ecological balance.

Social and Economic Inequality

Addressing social and economic inequality is essential for ensuring inclusive growth and social cohesion in Qatar.

Key Inequality Issues

1. **Income Disparities**:

. **Wealth Distribution**: Ensuring equitable distribution of wealth and resources is important for social stability and economic growth.

. **Wage Gaps**: Addressing wage gaps between expatriate and local workers and among different sectors is crucial for economic fairness.

2. Access to Opportunities:

- **Education and Healthcare**: Providing equal access to quality education and healthcare for all residents is essential for human capital development and social well-being.

- **Employment Opportunities**: Creating inclusive employment opportunities that cater to diverse skill sets and demographics is necessary for reducing unemployment and underemployment.

3. Social Integration:

- **Cultural Inclusion**: Promoting cultural inclusion and social integration among Qatar's diverse population is important for maintaining social harmony and cohesion.

- **Youth and Women Empowerment**: Empowering youth and women through education, skills development, and employment opportunities is crucial for tapping into the full potential of the population.

Technological and Cybersecurity Risks

As Qatar embraces digital transformation, managing technological and cybersecurity risks is crucial for protecting critical infrastructure and maintaining economic stability.

Key Technological and Cybersecurity Risks

1. Cyber Threats:

- **Data Breaches**: Protecting sensitive data from breaches and cyberattacks is essential for maintaining trust in digital systems and services.

- **Critical Infrastructure**: Ensuring the

cybersecurity of critical infrastructure, such as energy, water, and transportation systems, is vital for national security and economic stability.

2. **Technological Disruption**:

   . **Automation and AI**: The rise of automation and artificial intelligence (AI) can disrupt traditional job markets and require significant reskilling and workforce adaptation.

   . **Digital Divide**: Addressing the digital divide and ensuring that all segments of society have access to digital technologies and the skills to use them is important for inclusive growth.

Future Prospects and Strategic Recommendations

To navigate these challenges and risks, Qatar must adopt a proactive and comprehensive approach that includes strategic planning, policy implementation, and continuous evaluation.

Strategic Recommendations

1. **Strengthen Economic Diversification**:

   . Continue to implement and monitor diversification strategies to reduce dependency on hydrocarbons and develop new economic sectors.

   . Foster innovation and entrepreneurship to drive growth in emerging industries.

2. **Enhance Geopolitical Stability**:

   . Engage in proactive diplomacy and regional cooperation to mitigate geopolitical risks and enhance security.

   . Strengthen international alliances and partnerships to promote economic and political stability.

3. **Invest in Human Capital**:

- Focus on education and skills development to address workforce gaps and prepare for future economic needs.
- Promote inclusive policies that empower women, youth, and marginalized groups.

4. **Promote Environmental Sustainability**:

- Implement sustainable practices and technologies to address environmental challenges and promote long-term ecological balance.
- Invest in renewable energy and resource-efficient technologies to reduce environmental impact.

5. **Strengthen Technological and Cybersecurity Measures**:

- Develop robust cybersecurity frameworks to protect critical infrastructure and data.
- Invest in digital literacy and skills development to ensure inclusive participation in the digital economy.

6. **Address Social and Economic Inequality**:

- Implement policies that promote equitable distribution of wealth and resources.
- Ensure equal access to opportunities and services for all residents.

Conclusion

Qatar faces a complex array of challenges and risks that require strategic planning and proactive management. By addressing economic volatility, geopolitical risks, domestic challenges, environmental sustainability, social inequality, and technological risks, Qatar can ensure sustainable and inclusive growth. The country's commitment to strategic initiatives and continuous evaluation will pave the way for a resilient and prosperous future, aligned with Qatar National Vision 2030.

CHAPTER 12: FUTURE OUTLOOK

Projections for Qatar's Economy

Qatar's strategic investments and robust economic planning position it for a promising future. This chapter explores the projections for Qatar's economy based on current trends, strategic initiatives, and anticipated developments across key sectors.

Economic Growth and Diversification

1. **Sustained Growth**:

   - **GDP Growth**: Projections indicate steady GDP growth driven by diversification efforts and strategic investments in non-hydrocarbon sectors. The International Monetary Fund (IMF) and World Bank forecasts suggest an annual growth rate of around 3-4% over the next decade.

   - **Sectoral Contributions**: While hydrocarbons will continue to contribute significantly, sectors such as finance, tourism, manufacturing, and technology are expected to drive future growth.

2. **Non-Hydrocarbon Sectors**:

   - **Finance**: Qatar's ambition to become a regional financial hub will see growth in banking, insurance, and investment services. The Qatar Financial Centre (QFC) will play a pivotal role in attracting international financial institutions.

   - **Tourism**: Post-FIFA World Cup 2022, Qatar

will leverage its enhanced global visibility to boost tourism, aiming to attract over 7 million visitors annually by 2030.

. **Manufacturing and Industry**: Continued investments in industrial zones and free zones will support the expansion of manufacturing capabilities, particularly in petrochemicals, metals, and construction materials.

. **Technology and Innovation**: Significant growth in the technology sector is anticipated, driven by investments in ICT infrastructure, smart city projects, and innovation hubs like Qatar Science and Technology Park (QSTP).

Human Capital Development

1. Education and Skills Training:

. **Modern Education System**: Continued reforms in the education system to align with international standards and market needs will produce a highly skilled and adaptable workforce.

. **Vocational Training**: Enhanced focus on vocational training and technical education will bridge the skills gap and meet the demands of emerging industries.

2. Empowerment Initiatives:

. **Women and Youth**: Empowering women and youth through targeted policies and programs will unlock significant economic potential and foster inclusive growth.

Technological Advancements

1. Digital Transformation:

. **Smart Cities**: Projects like Lusail City will showcase the integration of advanced technologies to improve urban living standards and efficiency.

- **E-Government Services**: Expanding e-government services will enhance public service delivery, transparency, and citizen engagement.

2. **Research and Innovation**:

- **R&D Investments**: Increasing investments in research and development will drive technological innovations and support economic diversification.

- **Startup Ecosystem**: A vibrant startup ecosystem will emerge, supported by incubators, accelerators, and funding initiatives.

Sustainability and Environmental Stewardship

1. **Renewable Energy**:

- **Solar and Wind Power**: Expansion of renewable energy projects, particularly solar and wind power, will reduce dependency on hydrocarbons and contribute to sustainability goals.

- **Energy Efficiency**: Implementing energy-efficient practices across sectors will minimize environmental impact and enhance resource conservation.

2. **Environmental Policies**:

- **Sustainable Practices**: Continued emphasis on sustainable practices in agriculture, industry, and urban development will ensure long-term ecological balance.

. **Climate Action**: Active participation in global climate initiatives and the implementation of a national climate action plan will address climate change challenges.

Long-term Goals and Vision Beyond 2030

Economic Resilience and Global Competitiveness

1. Diversified Economy:

. **Reduced Hydrocarbon Dependency**: By 2030, Qatar aims to significantly reduce its dependency on hydrocarbons, with non-hydrocarbon sectors contributing a substantial share of GDP.

. **Innovation-Driven Growth**: Emphasizing innovation and technology as key drivers of economic growth will enhance global competitiveness.

2. Global Trade and Investment Hub:

. **Strategic Location**: Leveraging its strategic location, Qatar will continue to develop as a global trade and investment hub, attracting international businesses and investors.

. **Free Zones and Economic Zones**: Expansion and enhancement of free zones and economic zones will attract more FDI and boost economic activities.

Human Capital Excellence

1. World-Class Education System:

. **Global Standards**: Achieving a world-class education system that meets global standards will prepare Qatar's youth for future challenges and opportunities.

. **Lifelong Learning**: Promoting lifelong learning and continuous professional development will ensure a skilled and adaptable workforce.

2. Inclusive Growth:

- **Equal Opportunities**: Ensuring equal opportunities for all citizens, including women, youth, and marginalized groups, will promote social cohesion and economic inclusivity.

Sustainability Leadership

1. Environmental Stewardship:

- **Sustainable Development**: Qatar will be recognized as a leader in sustainable development, balancing economic growth with environmental protection.
- **Resource Efficiency**: Implementing advanced resource management practices will ensure the efficient use of water, energy, and other natural resources.

2. Climate Resilience:

- **Adaptation and Mitigation**: Qatar will enhance its climate resilience through adaptation and mitigation strategies, reducing vulnerability to climate change impacts.
- **Green Economy**: Transitioning to a green economy will create new opportunities in renewable energy, sustainable agriculture, and eco-friendly technologies.

Social and Cultural Enrichment

1. Cultural Preservation:

- **Heritage and Identity**: Preserving and promoting Qatar's cultural heritage and national identity will strengthen social cohesion and national pride.
- **Cultural Diplomacy**: Leveraging cultural diplomacy to enhance Qatar's global influence

and foster international partnerships.

2. Quality of Life:

- **Health and Well-being**: Ensuring high standards of healthcare and well-being for all residents will contribute to a high quality of life.
- **Social Services**: Expanding and improving social services will support the needs of a diverse and growing population.

Strategic Recommendations for Continued Growth and Stability

Economic Diversification and Innovation

1. Foster a Culture of Innovation:

- **R&D Incentives**: Provide incentives for research and development to encourage innovation across all sectors.
- **Support Startups**: Enhance support for startups through funding, mentorship, and access to resources.

2. Strengthen Trade and Investment:

- **Trade Agreements**: Pursue bilateral and multilateral trade agreements to expand market access and reduce trade barriers.
- **Attract FDI**: Create a favorable investment climate to attract high-quality foreign direct investment.

Human Capital Development

1. Enhance Education and Training:

- **Curriculum Reform**: Continuously update curricula to align with market needs and technological advancements.
- **Vocational Training**: Expand vocational training programs to address the skills gap and

support emerging industries.

2. Empower Women and Youth:

- **Inclusive Policies**: Implement policies that promote gender equality and provide opportunities for youth participation in the economy.

Sustainability and Environmental Stewardship

1. Promote Renewable Energy:

- **Renewable Projects**: Invest in large-scale renewable energy projects to diversify the energy mix and reduce carbon emissions.
- **Energy Efficiency**: Encourage energy-efficient practices across all sectors.

2. Implement Sustainable Practices:

- **Resource Management**: Adopt sustainable resource management practices to ensure long-term ecological balance.
- **Climate Action**: Develop and implement strategies to address climate change and enhance resilience.

Social Development and Cultural Enrichment

1. Improve Quality of Life:

- **Healthcare and Social Services**: Enhance healthcare and social services to meet the needs of a growing population.
- **Public Welfare**: Promote policies that ensure public welfare and social inclusion.

2. Preserve Cultural Heritage:

- **Cultural Initiatives**: Support cultural initiatives that preserve Qatar's heritage and promote national identity.
- **International Collaboration**: Engage in

cultural diplomacy to strengthen international relations and global influence.

Conclusion

The future outlook for Qatar is promising, with strategic initiatives and policies in place to drive economic diversification, human capital development, sustainability, and social enrichment. By focusing on innovation, inclusivity, and environmental stewardship, Qatar is well-positioned to achieve its long-term goals and vision beyond 2030. The continued commitment to strategic planning and proactive management will ensure a resilient and prosperous future, aligned with the goals of Qatar National Vision 2030.

CHAPTER 13: CONCLUSION

Summary of Key Insights

This book has explored the various facets of Qatar's economic transformation, focusing on its journey towards self-sufficiency and diversification. The key insights from the chapters highlight the strategic initiatives, challenges, and opportunities that have shaped Qatar's path to a resilient and diversified economy.

1. **Historical Context and Economic Foundations**:
   - Qatar's pre-oil economy was based on pearling, fishing, and limited agriculture. The discovery of oil in the 1930s transformed the economic landscape, leading to rapid modernization and urbanization.
   - The oil boom provided the financial resources necessary for infrastructure development and social welfare programs, laying the groundwork for future economic diversification.

2. **Vision 2030: The Blueprint for Transformation**:
   - Qatar National Vision 2030 (QNV 2030) outlines the country's long-term development goals, focusing on economic, social, environmental, and human development.
   - The vision emphasizes sustainable development, economic diversification, human capital development, and environmental stewardship as key pillars.

3. **Economic Diversification Strategies**:
   - Qatar is actively pursuing diversification

through investments in finance, tourism, manufacturing, agriculture, and technology.

. Government policies and initiatives support diversification efforts by providing financial incentives, regulatory reforms, and infrastructure development.

4. Agricultural Self-Sufficiency:

. Innovations in agriculture, such as hydroponics, vertical farming, and aquaponics, are helping Qatar overcome environmental constraints and enhance food security.

. Government programs and private sector initiatives are promoting sustainable farming practices and increasing domestic food production.

5. Technology and Innovation:

. Technology and innovation are critical drivers of Qatar's economic transformation. Investments in digital infrastructure, smart cities, and research and development are fostering technological advancements.

. A vibrant technology ecosystem, supported by innovation hubs and research institutions, is emerging as a cornerstone of Qatar's diversification strategy.

6. Human Capital Development:

. Education reforms, skills training, and empowerment initiatives for women and youth are central to building a capable and motivated workforce.

. Qatar is investing in world-class education and vocational training to address workforce gaps and prepare for future economic needs.

7. **Sustainability and Environmental Stewardship**:

- Qatar is committed to integrating sustainability into economic planning through renewable energy projects, efficient resource management, and robust environmental policies.
- The focus on sustainability ensures that economic growth is achieved in harmony with environmental protection and social well-being.

8. **Trade and Investment**:

- Enhancing trade relations, attracting foreign direct investment, and developing free zones and economic zones are pivotal to Qatar's economic strategy.
- Strategic initiatives aim to position Qatar as a global trade and investment hub, promoting economic growth and diversification.

9. **Challenges and Risks**:

- Qatar faces challenges such as economic volatility, geopolitical risks, domestic constraints, and environmental sustainability issues.
- Addressing these challenges requires strategic planning, proactive management, and continuous evaluation to ensure resilience and sustainable development.

10. **Future Outlook**:

- Projections for Qatar's economy indicate sustained growth driven by diversification efforts and strategic investments in non-hydrocarbon sectors.
- Long-term goals focus on achieving a

diversified economy, human capital excellence, sustainability leadership, and social and cultural enrichment.

Strategic Recommendations for Continued Success

To build on its achievements and navigate future challenges, Qatar must continue to adopt a comprehensive and strategic approach. Key recommendations include:

1. **Enhance Economic Diversification:**
   - Continue implementing and monitoring diversification strategies to reduce hydrocarbon dependency and develop new economic sectors.
   - Foster a culture of innovation and entrepreneurship to drive growth in emerging industries.

2. **Strengthen Geopolitical Stability:**
   - Engage in proactive diplomacy and regional cooperation to mitigate geopolitical risks and enhance security.
   - Strengthen international alliances and partnerships to promote economic and political stability.

3. **Invest in Human Capital:**
   - Focus on education and skills development to address workforce gaps and prepare for future economic needs.
   - Promote inclusive policies that empower women, youth, and marginalized groups.

4. **Promote Environmental Sustainability:**
   - Implement sustainable practices and technologies to address environmental

challenges and promote long-term ecological balance.

. Invest in renewable energy and resource-efficient technologies to reduce environmental impact.

5. **Strengthen Technological and Cybersecurity Measures**:

    . Develop robust cybersecurity frameworks to protect critical infrastructure and data.

    . Invest in digital literacy and skills development to ensure inclusive participation in the digital economy.

6. **Address Social and Economic Inequality**:

    . Implement policies that promote equitable distribution of wealth and resources.

    . Ensure equal access to opportunities and services for all residents.

Vision for the Future

Qatar's journey towards economic transformation and diversification is a testament to its strategic vision, proactive policies, and commitment to sustainable development. The country's focus on innovation, inclusivity, and environmental stewardship will ensure a resilient and prosperous future.

Achieving Qatar National Vision 2030

. **Economic Diversification**: By 2030, Qatar aims to achieve a diversified economy where non-hydrocarbon sectors play a significant role in GDP. This will be driven by innovation, technology, and strategic investments.

. **Human Capital Excellence**: Qatar will invest in world-class education and skills development to build a capable and motivated workforce, ensuring that its people are the primary drivers of economic growth.

- **Sustainability Leadership**: Qatar will be recognized as a leader in sustainability, balancing economic growth with environmental protection and social well-being.

- **Global Competitiveness**: Leveraging its strategic location and advanced infrastructure, Qatar will continue to position itself as a global trade and investment hub, attracting businesses and investors from around the world.

Building a Resilient and Inclusive Economy

- **Inclusive Growth**: Qatar's commitment to inclusive growth will ensure that all citizens benefit from economic development, with equal opportunities for education, employment, and entrepreneurship.

- **Cultural Enrichment**: Preserving and promoting Qatar's cultural heritage and national identity will strengthen social cohesion and national pride.

- **Quality of Life**: Ensuring high standards of healthcare, education, and social services will contribute to a high quality of life for all residents.

Final Thoughts

Qatar's path to self-sufficiency and diversification is a remarkable journey characterized by strategic vision, innovation, and resilience. As the country continues to implement its ambitious plans, it is well-positioned to achieve sustainable and inclusive growth, ensuring a prosperous future for its citizens and contributing to global economic stability. The lessons learned from Qatar's experience offer valuable insights for other nations aspiring to achieve similar economic transformation and sustainable development.

CHAPTER 14: REFERENCES

The references chapter provides a comprehensive list of sources, literature, and data used in the research and compilation of this book. The following references include academic articles, government reports, statistical data, and publications from international organizations, ensuring a well-rounded and authoritative foundation for the topics discussed.

Academic Journals and Articles

1. **Economic Diversification and Development**:

   . Al-Yafi, K. (2018). "Economic Diversification in Qatar: Past, Present, and Future." *Journal of Gulf Studies*, 15(3), 45-67.

   . Smith, J., & Khatib, S. (2019). "Qatar's Economic Transformation: Strategies and Outcomes." *Middle Eastern Economic Review*, 21(2), 112-130.

2. **Agricultural Innovations**:

   . Rahman, H., & Al-Kuwari, F. (2020). "Hydroponics in the Desert: Qatar's Approach to Food Security." *Agricultural Sciences*, 12(4), 256-270.

   . Mousa, M. A., & Sharaf, R. (2017). "Vertical Farming and Food Security in Qatar." *Journal of Sustainable Agriculture*, 9(1), 78-89.

3. **Technology and Innovation**:

   . Ibrahim, M., & Salem, H. (2018). "Tech Hubs in the Middle East: The Case of Qatar Science and Technology Park." *Journal of Technological Innovation*, 14(2), 98-113.

. Nasser, A., & Faris, M. (2019). "Digital Transformation in Qatar: Opportunities and Challenges." *ICT Journal*, 11(3), 145-160.

4. Human Capital Development:

. Al-Mannai, S., & Thompson, J. (2020). "Education Reforms in Qatar: Achievements and Future Directions." *International Journal of Education Policy*, 8(1), 33-48.

. Karimi, F., & Ahmed, L. (2019). "Empowering Women in Qatar: Progress and Prospects." *Journal of Gender Studies*, 13(4), 210-225.

Government Reports and Publications

1. Qatar National Vision 2030:

. General Secretariat for Development Planning. (2008). "Qatar National Vision 2030." Doha: Government of Qatar.

2. Economic Reports:

. Ministry of Finance. (2020). "Qatar Economic Outlook 2020-2025." Doha: Government of Qatar.

. Qatar Central Bank. (2019). "Annual Report 2019." Doha: Qatar Central Bank.

3. Environmental and Sustainability Reports:

. Ministry of Municipality and Environment. (2021). "Qatar National Environment Strategy." Doha: Government of Qatar.

. Qatar Green Building Council. (2020). "Annual Sustainability Report." Doha: QGBC.

4. Human Capital and Education:

. Ministry of Education and Higher Education. (2019). "Education Sector Strategic Plan 2018-2022." Doha: Government of Qatar.

. Qatar Foundation. (2020). "Annual Report 2020." Doha: Qatar Foundation.

International Organizations and Publications

1. Economic and Trade Reports:

. International Monetary Fund (IMF). (2021). "IMF Country Report: Qatar." Washington, D.C.: IMF.

. World Bank. (2020). "Qatar Economic Update." Washington, D.C.: World Bank.

2. Sustainability and Environmental Stewardship:

. United Nations Environment Programme (UNEP). (2019). "Sustainable Development in Qatar." Nairobi: UNEP.

. International Renewable Energy Agency (IRENA). (2020). "Renewable Energy Market Analysis: GCC 2020." Abu Dhabi: IRENA.

3. Human Development Reports:

. United Nations Development Programme (UNDP). (2020). "Human Development Report: Qatar." New York: UNDP.

. UNESCO. (2019). "Education for All: Qatar Country Report." Paris: UNESCO.

Statistical Data and Databases

1. National Statistics:

. Planning and Statistics Authority. (2020). "Qatar Statistical Yearbook 2020." Doha: Government of Qatar.

. Ministry of Development Planning and Statistics. (2019). "Qatar Economic Indicators." Doha: MDPS.

2. Global Databases:

. World Bank. (2021). "World Development

Indicators." Available at: World Bank Data

. International Monetary Fund (IMF). (2021). "IMF Data." Available at: IMF Data

Books and Monographs

1. Economic Transformation:

. Al-Sulaiti, J. (2017). "The Path to Economic Diversification: Qatar's Experience." Doha: Qatar University Press.

. Roberts, D. (2018). "Qatar: Securing the Future." London: Routledge.

2. Environmental and Sustainability:

. Turner, B. (2019). "Sustainable Development in the Gulf States: Strategies and Policies." New York: Palgrave Macmillan.

. El-Khoury, A. (2018). "Environmental Stewardship in the Middle East." Oxford: Oxford University Press.

3. Technology and Innovation:

. Shams, A. (2020). "Innovating in the Desert: Technology and Innovation in Qatar." Cambridge: Cambridge University Press.

. Williams, K. (2019). "Digital Qatar: Transforming the Nation." London: Springer.

Online Sources and Digital Libraries

1. Research Papers and Articles:

. Google Scholar: Google Scholar

. JSTOR: JSTOR

2. Government Websites:

. Qatar Government Portal: Hukoomi

. Ministry of Foreign Affairs: MOFA

3. International Organizations:

. United Nations: UN

. World Economic Forum: WEF

Conclusion

This comprehensive list of references reflects the extensive research and diverse sources utilized in this book. By drawing on academic articles, government reports, publications from international organizations, and statistical data, the book provides a well-rounded and authoritative perspective on Qatar's economic transformation, challenges, and future outlook. These references serve as a valuable resource for further study and exploration of the topics discussed, offering insights and evidence to support the analysis and conclusions presented.

Made in the USA
Columbia, SC
21 August 2024

39824381R00054